DO YOU WANT A PET HEDGEHOG?

THAT'S AN ODD PET!

Enslow PUBLISHING

BY LOUIS MALLORY

Please visit our website, www.enslow.com. For a free color catalog of all our high-quality books, call toll free 1-800-398-2504 or fax 1-877-980-4454.

Cataloging-in-Publication Data

Names: Mallory, Louis.
Title: Do you want a pet hedgehog? / Louis Mallory.
Description: Buffalo, NY : Enslow Publishing, 2025. | Series: That's an odd pet! | Includes glossary and index.
Identifiers: ISBN 9781978540804 (pbk.) | ISBN 9781978540811 (library bound) | ISBN 9781978540828 (ebook)
Subjects: LCSH: Hedgehogs as pets–Juvenile literature. | Hedgehogs–Juvenile literature.
Classification: LCC SF459.H43 M35 2025 | DDC 636.933'22–dc23

Published in 2025 by
Enslow Publishing
2544 Clinton Street
Buffalo, NY 14224

Portions of this work were originally authored by Melissa Raé Shofner and published as *Hedgehogs*. All new material in this edition is authored by Louis Mallory.

Designer: Claire Zimmermann
Editor: Natalie Humphrey

Photo credits: Cover (photo) Sebastian Duda/Shutterstock.com; Series Art (title and heading font, texture) Gleb Guralnyk/Shutterstock.com; Series Art (background retro swirl) ChekmanDaria/Shutterstock.com; Series Art (corner dots) Romanova Ekaterina/Shutterstock.com; Series Art (body text boxes, page number background shape) Angie Makes/Shutterstock.com; Series Art (hand-drawn doodles) yugoro/Shutterstock.com; p. 5 supakrit tirayasupasin/Shutterstock.com; pp. 7, 19 Anne Coatesy/Shutterstock.com; p. 9 dimid_86/Shutterstock.com; p. 11 Jenn Huls/Shutterstock.com; p. 13 lara-sh/Shutterstock.com; p. 15 Maximilian100/Shutterstock.com; p. 17 ALIAKSANDR PALCHEUSKI/Shutterstock.com.

Printed in the United States of America

CPSIA compliance information: Batch #CSENS25: For further information contact Enslow Publishing at 1-800-398-2504.

CONTENTS

Words in the glossary appear in **bold** type the first time they are used in the text.

ODD ANIMALS

With a body covered in **quills**, hedgehogs might not be the softest pet around. But this odd pet is the perfect friend for many pet owners. Hedgehogs, also called hedgies, are becoming more popular. These little pets are known for being curious, funny, and a whole lot of fun!

JUST THE FACTS!

It is illegal to own hedgehogs in Georgia; Hawaii; California; Pennsylvania; Washington, DC; and in New York City.

A hedgehog's back is covered in quills, but its face, legs, and belly have soft fur.

But before you run out and pick up your own hedgehog, make sure you can own them in your state. Hedgehogs are legal to own in most states, but not all.

WILD HEDGEHOGS

Wild hedgehogs can be found throughout Asia, Europe, and Africa. They live in many different **habitats**. They live in deserts, forests, and even cities. Hedgehogs are mostly nocturnal, which means they sleep during the day and are awake at night.

Some hedgehogs dig **burrows**. Hedgehog burrows can be up to 20 inches (51 cm) deep. Hedgehogs that don't dig burrows usually make nests. Their nests can be made of leaves, grasses, and branches.

Wild hedgehogs usually live alone. Pet hedgehogs should be kept alone too!

JUST THE FACTS!

There are many different species, or kinds, of wild hedgehog.

EATING BUGS

Wild hedgehogs eat worms, beetles, slugs, and many other bugs. For your pet hedgehog, pet stores sell special food. This food has everything your pet needs to stay healthy. Certain cat foods are also an option for your hedgehog's **diet**.

JUST THE FACTS!

Hedgehogs can also eat certain fruits and vegetables as a treat. Always check with your hedgie's vet to make sure your hedgie's food is good for it!

Some bugs, like crickets and mealworms, make great treats for your hedgehog!

Make sure your hedgehog always has fresh water. Use a small, heavy bowl so your pet can't tip it over. Some hedgehog owners hang a special water bottle in their hedgie's cage instead.

A HEDGIE'S HOME

Hedgehogs need a cage big enough for them to play in. A cage at least 2 by 3 feet (61 by 91 cm) is usually a good size. Some hedgehogs can learn to use a **litter box** to go to the bathroom, but others can be messier.

JUST THE FACTS!

Only use warm water in a shallow dish to bathe your hedgie! Never use scented soaps or make the water too deep for them to stand in.

You can use a soft toothbrush to safely clean your hedgehog.

Hedgehogs don't **groom** themselves like many other animals. That means pet hedgehogs need a bath about once a month. If your hedgehog is dirty or has dry skin, it's time for a bath!

HOLDING YOUR HEDGEHOG

Learning how to hold your hedgie is an important part of owning a hedgehog. Getting poked by a hedgehog's quills may feel like touching a cactus.

Your pet isn't trying to hurt you. It's trying to stay safe. When attacked, hedgehogs curl up in a ball, making their quills stick out. This hurts predators and keeps them from attacking the hedgehog. When your hedgie becomes comfortable around you, it won't roll up and poke you as much.

Hedgehog quills are made of the same **material** your hair and fingernails are made of: keratin!

JUST THE FACTS!

To hold your hedgehog, let them sniff your hand first. Then, gently cup your hands and hold your hedgehog gently underneath its belly.

ARE THEY REALLY HOGS?

Even though they have "hog" in their name, hedgehogs are the cousins of moonrats, shrews, and moles. They aren't related to pigs at all! Hedgehogs probably got their name because of how they **forage**. They search through **hedges** and other plants to find food. When doing this, hedgehogs sometimes grunt or sound like pigs.

JUST THE FACTS!

Hedgehogs can have a lot of teeth. The average hedgie can have up to 44 teeth!

Because of their appearance, some people think hedgehogs are related to porcupines. However, the only thing these animals have in common is their quills!

VISITING THE VET

To keep your hedgehog healthy, you should take your hedgie to a vet for a yearly checkup.

Hedgehogs can get mites. Mites are **parasites** that can bite your hedgehog and make it sick. If your hedgehog starts losing a lot of its quills or you see it scratching or licking its body a lot, it may have mites. Tell an adult and make sure your hedgehog is taken to the vet.

If you notice your hedgehog acting differently than it usually does, tell an adult! This can include a lot of scratching, or rubbing its skin with its claws to stop an itch.

JUST THE FACTS!

Hedgehogs can get mites from another hedgehog with mites or bedding **infested** with them.

HIBERNATION

In the wild, hedgehogs will hibernate during the colder months of the year. Hibernating is when an animal enters a sleep-like state for a long period of time, usually during the winter. When the weather gets cold, hedgehogs make themselves comfortable in their nests and stay there until spring.

JUST THE FACTS!

To learn more about hibernation and if it's safe for your hedgehog, talk to your hedgehog's vet. Ask any questions you may have.

Hedgehogs may slow down when it gets to be below 60°F (15.5°C).

As pets, hedgehogs may try to hibernate if they get too cold. Pet hedgehogs don't need to hibernate though! Hibernation can cause problems, such as sickness, in some hedgehogs.

FRIENDLY HEDGEHOGS

If you take care of your hedgie, not only will it live longer, but it can be a great friend too! Pet hedgehogs usually live between four and six years. But with the right care, your hedgie may live more than eight years.

While hedgehogs should be kept alone, many hedgehogs enjoy spending time with their owners. Regularly playing with your hedgehog, giving it toys, and spending time with it can help your hedgehog bond, or connect, with you.

TAKING CARE OF YOUR HEDGEHOG!

Feed your hedgehog hedgehog food and make sure it always has fresh water.

Give your hedgehog crickets, mealworms, fruits, and vegetables as special treats. Only give it a few!

Deep clean your hedgehog's cage once a week and spot clean daily.

If your hedgie uses a litter box, make sure to clean it regularly.

Give your hedgehog toys, tubes, and an exercise wheel to play with.

Hold your hedgehog carefully so it doesn't poke you.

Bring your hedgie to the vet once a year.

JUST THE FACTS!

Many hedgehogs enjoy running on wheels and playing in tunnels or mazes. For an active hedgie, even a toilet-paper tube can make a fun toy!

GLOSSARY

burrow: A hole in the ground an animal uses to live or hide in.

diet: The food that an animal eats.

forage: To hunt or search for something, such as food.

groom: To clean.

habitat: The natural place where an animal or plant lives.

hedge: A row of bushes often used as a boundary.

infest: To overrun a place in large numbers and become harmful or unpleasant.

litter box: A box holding a dry material called litter that some animals use as a toilet indoors.

material: Matter from which something is made.

parasite: A living thing that lives in, on, or with another living thing, causing harm.

quill: A long, sharp, thin spine.

FOR MORE INFORMATION

Books

Brandle, Marie. *Hedgehogs*. Minneapolis, MN: Tadpole Books, 2024.

Rice, Jamie. *Hedgehog or Porcupine?*. Minneapolis, MN: Jump!, Inc, 2023.

Websites

Britannica Kids: Hedgehog
kids.britannica.com/kids/article/hedgehog/391021
Find out more information about wild hedgehogs.

National Geographic Kids: Hedgehog
kids.nationalgeographic.com/animals/mammals/facts/hedgehog
Learn more about how hedgehogs live in the wild.

INDEX